The Tri-Spired Gem:
Holy Family Cathedral

a collection of essays,
diaries, and reflections

edited by Michael A. Malcom

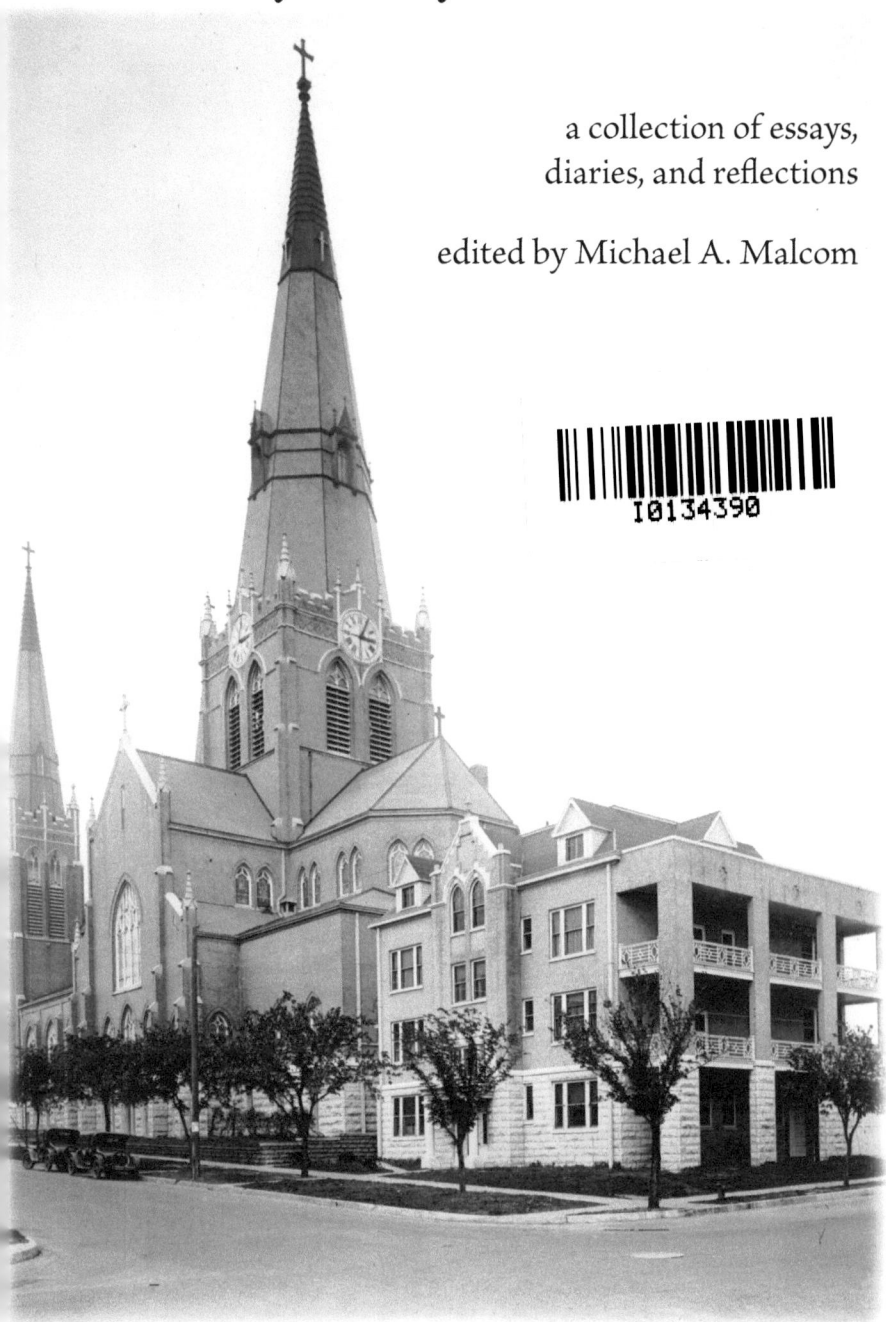

I0134390

Editor's Note:

I compiled *The Tri-Spired Gem* at the request of the 2014 Centennial Committee. It is a forum for a number of essays written about various aspects of parish life at the Cathedral, notable moments in our history, and a glimpse at the character of some of Holy Family's parishioners and clergy.

I am including excerpts from the diaries of two of the parish's first pastors. Not only do they provide historical details recorded nowhere else, but they give us insight into the trials of parish priests in the American prairie. I have special affection for Father John Heiring, the parish's third priest, who built the church we know as Holy Family Cathedral before he celebrated his 40th birthday. He called Holy Family *The Tri-Spired Gem of Catholicity*.

Near the end of this short book is a brief description of the four iterations of the church's interior, with a slightly less brief look back at some of the recent work done.

I must thank Jane Sloan for her tireless work combing through hundreds of newspaper articles to help me with researching Holy Family's history, Cathy Nelson for taking nearly 10,000 photos for me in the last seventeen years, and Monsignor Gregory Gier for giving me both constructive advice and creative freedom.

Mike Malcom

Dedication:

This book is dedicated to two Catholics who graced Holy Family Cathedral with their presence: **Blessed Teresa of Calcutta** and **Father Stan Rother**.

Mother Teresa visited Tulsa on May 11, 1976 as part of a tour of the United States designed to raise awareness of the plight of the poor in India. After attending a Tuesday evening Mass at the Cathedral, she spoke at the Tulsa Civic Center. The next morning she returned to Holy Family, went to Mass, and departed Tulsa to continue her nationwide tour.

Father Stanley Rother was the Associate Pastor of Holy Family in 1966. He lived in the Rectory and often taught in Holy Family School. He served a number of parishes, including Saint James the Apostle Parish in Santiago Atitlan, Guatemala. In 1981, after his name had appeared on a death list, he was shot and killed in his rectory. He was one of ten priests murdered in Guatemala that year.

Father Rother is a Servant of God, meaning that the cause for his canonization is open. The Vatican is reviewing documentation submitted by the Archdiocese of Oklahoma City.

My dear Co-Workers,
Let us become a true and fruitful branch on the vine, Jesus, by accepting Him in our lives as it pleases Him to come-
as the Truth - to be told; as the life-to be lived
as the Light - to be lighted; as the Love-to be loved
as the Way - to be walked; as the Joy-to be given
as the Peace - to be spread; as the Sacrifice -to be offered
in our families and with our close neighbors as well as our far-away neighbors.

God bless you,

M. Teresa mc

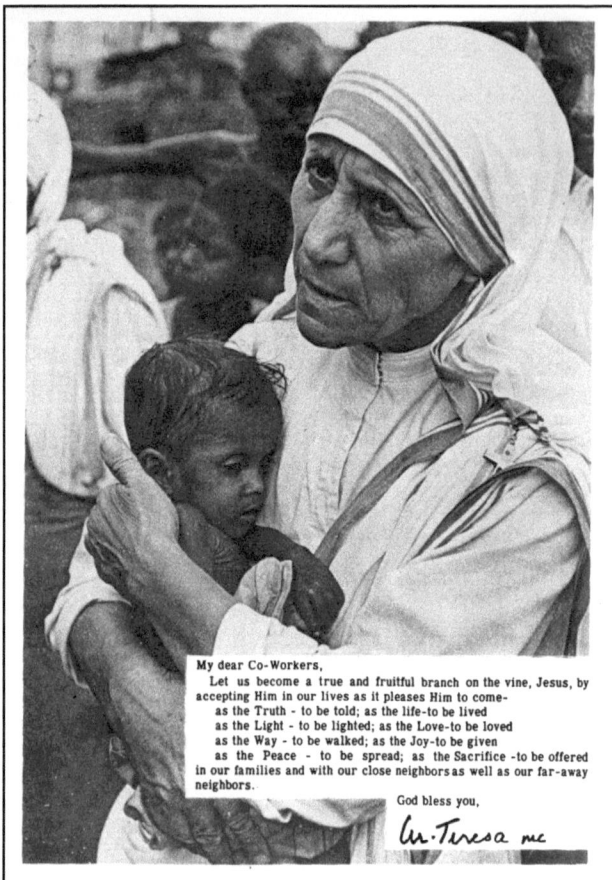

Blessed Teresa of Calcutta

visited Tulsa in May of 1976.
She attended Mass twice at Holy Family Cathedral.
When she was here, she gave away prayer cards (above)
and offered this prayer:

Make us worthy, Lord to serve our fellow men throughout the world who live and die in poverty and hunger. Give them, through our hands, this day their daily bread, and by our understanding love give peace and joy. Amen.

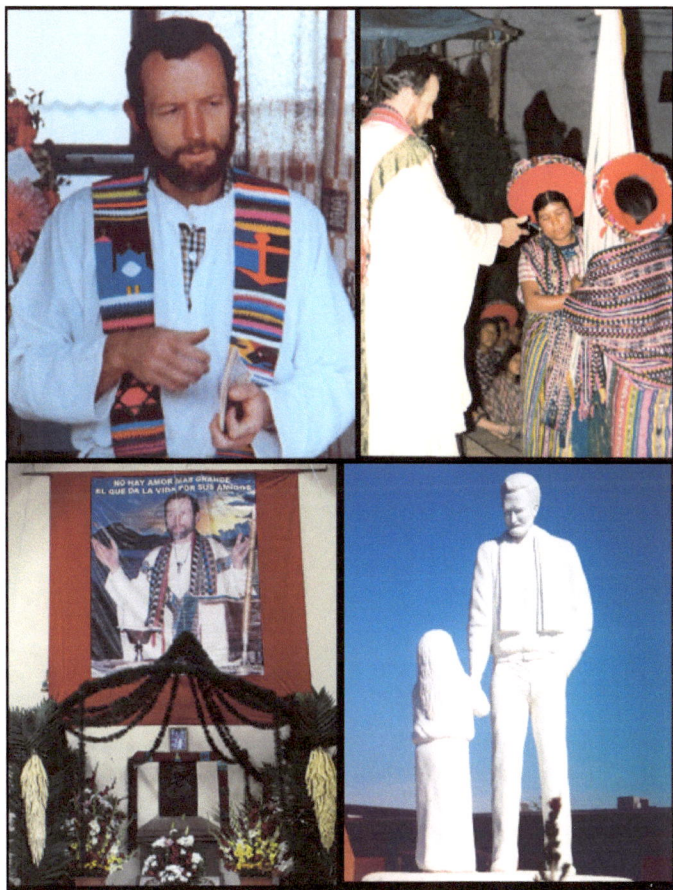

Prayer for the Cause of Canonization of Servant of God
Father Stanley Rother

O God, fount of all holiness, make us each walk worthily in our vocation, through the intercession of your Saints, on whom you bestowed a great variety of graces on earth. Having graced Your Church with the life and ministry of your missionary priest Stanley Rother, grant that by his intercession this humble flock may reach where the brave Shepherd has gone. Grant that Your Church may proclaim him as Martyr and Saint serving in Your presence and interceding for us. Through Christ our Lord. Amen.

Table of Contents

The Van Hulse brothers, three biological brothers who were priests in Oklahoma.
Fathers Charles, Joseph, and Theophile Van Hulse (left to right)

Record of the Holy Family Church and Parish of Tulsa, Indian Territory

by Rev. Charles Van Hulse

About 7 years ago (which would be about 1890) Reverend Father W. Ketcham had been appointed pastor of Muskogee and the surrounding country. He found that in the little town of Tulsa, about 65 miles west of Muskogee, there were also a few Catholics. He visited the place from time to time, saying Mass in a house and seeing that the place likely would some day become a thriving town, he obtained, with the assistance of Rt. Rev. Bishop Meerschaert, from Mr. Perryman, at that time Chief of the tribe of Creek Indians, the permission to build a Catholic church in Tulsa. But the permission to build a church did not bring it there and so Father Ketcham and his successor, Father G. Depreitere, who visited Tulsa monthly from Oct. 1895 until Nov. 1897, continued to say Mass in a private dwelling house and as the congregation was very small, one room usually was large enough to contain the worshippers. From Nov. 1897, Tulsa was visited monthly by Rev. Charles Van Hulse, who, like his predecessors, was obliged to hold services in a private residence.

The Catholic people, though, began to speak about building a church. In the beginning of 1899 a subscription was opened and the success was beyond expectations of both priest and people. At the head of the list was Mr. & Mrs. L. Appleby, with a subscription of $500.00, followed by Mr. P. Coyle, with $150.00, Mr. & Mrs. Hoots, with $100.00 and Mr. & Mrs. Boyd, with $50.00. The Rt. Rev. Bishop Meerschaert also contributed $100.00. Then several other donations of $25.00, $10.00, $5.00, etc. given by other Catholics and by business men of Tulsa. In all, about $1,400.00 was collected.

Rev. Father Ketcham, several years before, had bought a lot on which to build a church, but as it was rather small, Rev. Charles Van Hulse exchanged it for a whole block, a little farther from the business part of town.

During the month of May, the contract was let for the building of a church that would cost about $1,500.00. That church was dedicated on Sunday, Sept. 10th, 1899. It is 60 feet long and 30 wide. A room of 10 ft. by 10 ft. is attached to it, serving as a sacristy and there it is also that the priest, Rev. Charles Van Hulse, made his home. The altar in the church is only temporary, put up by the priest, until a better one can be procured.

After about two months, owing to the donations of friends and relatives in Belgium, Europe, and giving his own money to the last cent, the priest succeeded in paying the debt of the church and in procuring suitable seats for it. In the meantime, also, a school building had been started. Rev. Mother Catherine [sic] Drexel and Rt. Rev. Bishop Meerschaert were the great benefactors who enabled the priest to put up a building as school and dwelling for the Sister-Teachers.

Three Sisters of Mount Carmel, from New Orleans, La. were engaged to come to teach. Unfortunately, the school was not finished and from the 11th day of Sept. 1899 until the first Monday in October, the Sisters taught in the church. Then, finally, they were about to move into the other building.

Although great efforts had been made by some bigots in Tulsa to prevent children from coming to that Catholic school, the number of enrolled pupils was above 80 and the whole year there was an average of 65 pupils, about 20 of whom were Catholics.

The school closed its first session on the 28th of May, 1900, with an entertainment given by the pupils and which showed clearly the progress they had made under the care and instructions of the sisters. One of the great good results also of the church and school both, was the First Communion of a class of 12 children on Easter Sunday, 1900. The Catholic congregation in Tulsa now numbered between fifty and sixty members.

A great many improvements, of course, are still needed for the church. As for the school building, although it is too small and not finished inside and notwithstanding the sacrifices that the priest has made, the whole year and his efforts to obtain more help, there is a debt on it yet of $750.00. May God inspire some wealthy person to enable us to cancel that debt and make some, at least of the most necessary improvements. Deo Gracias.

A Historical Sketch of Holy Family Parish

by Rev. Msgr. John G. Heiring

This population was made up, like well nigh all of them, of persons and families of various creeds and no creed. In this year 1894 Rev. W. Ketchum, who was the pastor of the Catholic congregation of Muskogee, I. T., and had in his charge the surrounding vicinity for miles in all directions, came to Tulsa and found among the inhabitants some sons and daughters from good Catholic homes, who though they had ventured far to the frontiers, had nevertheless brought with them that sacred inheritance of their faith. These were joyously glad when from time to time they were favored with the visit of the priest.

He would celebrate mass in the home of one or other and all would assemble there to assist in the sacred services. Entertaining the fond hope that in some future day they might have a little place of worship Rev. W. Ketchum with the cooperation of the Rt. Rev. Theophile Meerschaert, D. D. (bishop) secured the lot. At this time the Rt Rev. Bishop made his first visit to Tulsa and secured from Mr. Perryman, at that time chief of the Creek Indians, the permission to build a church. It was on April 25, 1895. His Lordship said mass in the room of the hotel and lectured at the arranged hour.

After that Tulsa Catholics were visited monthly from October 1895 until November, 1897, by Rev. G. Depreitere, the successor or rather the assistant of Rev. W. Ketchum.

All the while services were conducted in residences of the members. Rev. Charles Van Hulse followed Rev. G. Depreitere in administering to the faithful of Tulsa.

The original church lot was on the corner of Second Street and Cincinnati Ave. During the time of the Rev. Charles Van Hulse, this lot was disposed of and the block on Third and Elgin was purchased.

Rev. Charles Van Hulse raised funds by circulating a subscription list in the year 1899 and the contract for the church erection was let at a cost of $1500.00.

The church having been built, was dedicated on September 10th, 1899. It was 30 feet wide by 50 feet in length, with an apse for an altar. Attached thereto was a little room 10 feet by 10 feet, serving as sacristy and as home for Rev. Charles Van Hulse, who then became resident pastor.

The original church and school, established in September of 1899

In the exchange of sites the deed of possession shows that $400.00 were paid and later on payments were made to the Department of the Interior, U. S. Indian Service, until the deed was issued.

This left the church dedicated to the HOLY FAMILY, Jesus, Mary and Joseph, provided with proper site for future expansion. For the expansion the ground was laid in the fact that a school was planned at the same time the church was in building.

Inasmuch as there were many Indian children here within the village and about, it was projected as an Indian school.

The Rt. Rev. T. Meerschaert, Vicar Apostolic of Oklahoma and Indian Territories and Bishop of Sydima, conferred with Ven. Mother Catherine [sic] Drexel, who was then assisting many such projects for the benefit of the Indians and the colored races. She consented to advance $1,500 for the erection of the school, with the written agreement that, when this said school should cease to be an Indian school, the amount be refunded to her. This sum with further assistance of the Rt. Rev. Bishop completed the school. It was a frame structure 32 by 34 feet which served as school and at the same time as residence for the sisters.

Three Sisters of Mount Carmel from New Orleans had been secured and placed in charge of the school. The building, however, was not completed in time to open the school work therein by September. So classes were begun in the church and conducted therein from the 11th of September, 1899, until the first Monday in October, 1899. The average attendance was 65 pupils. The school closed its first scholastic year on the 28th day of May, 1900, with an entertainment given by the pupils showing splendid results having been achieved under the care and instruction of the good sisters.

Easter Sunday was especially a joyful day for the Holy Family congregation, for on this day the first class was admitted to the First Holy Communion. A class of eleven enjoyed this privilege. At this time the congregation numbered between 50 and 60 members.

Many further improvements were yet needed for the church. The school building also was not yet finished inside and there remained a debt pending of $750.00.

Ever since the time the Rev. Charles Van Hulse took up his residence in Tulsa, the little surrounding places were attended to from Tulsa. Thus Tulsa became the center from which the priest's ministrations for the people within a radius of from 25 to 50 miles emanated.

This continued during the incumbency of Rev. Theophile Van Hulse. He was active here from 1900 to 1906.

During this time the congregation increased in number. He succeeded in wiping out the remaining debt, besides completing interiorly and equipping the little school.

He also erected a parochial residence of four rooms, being two stories. This was indeed a great and needed improvement for it was quite impossible for a priest to subsist in the small room above described.

It was during his time that the Sisters of Divine Providence took charge of the school. This was in 1902.

The school was filled to capacity and it became necessary to add two small rooms serving as kitchen and dining room for the sisters.

In the Spring of 1906, on the 17th day of March, Council 1104 of the Knights of Columbus was launched with the initiation of Charter members.

The Rt. Rev. Bishop having confirmed a class on the same day in the morning remained for the conferring of the three degrees. This confirmation class was the third one to go on record in the Holy Family Parish.

The above described RED LETTER day, April 17th, 1906, when a large class was confirmed and when the charter members of the Council 1104 were initiated, was the fatal day for the writer. The writer was up to that time and five months later, unaware that such a place as Tulsa was on the map.

[Bishop Meerschaert's plan to make Father Heiring the pastor of the church in Tulsa] became an actuality in the Fall of the same year, i. e., 1906, October 30th.

On October the 29th, with less than two hours of this eventful day remaining, with the train so out of balance that the rear end coach was in the lead, and the world seemingly twisted on its axis, a crowd found the way out of the dimly kerosene-oil lighted coach following the porter, with an equally bright light, to the platform in front of that red painted type of early pioneer days Frisco depots. Among this crowd was the obedience-fettered victim.

It is an instance demonstrating how wise the decree of the almighty and benign God, when He made the future hidden from us.

Without narrating the story, suffice it to say that the purport of the story was this: His Lordship had been aiding the struggling little congregation to which the various missions were attached, in sustaining the physical life and existence of the priest in charge. This His Lordship did in many missions in the early days.

But on the 17th day of March by the supreme decree of his Lordship the writer was victimized, and by that same decree, that unwritten yet inviolable decision was made, that he would no more assist in supporting the priest of Holy Family Parish financially. Not knowing the future made impossible for me to divine that this was but a repetition of a like attempt at my former, and first appointment.

Besides the rats about the depot, for it was evident that plenty of these rodents were there by reason of the many rat-holes, there were also colored gentlemen, and in almost indiscernible darkness the first words of welcome in Tulsa came, in "Hotel, Sir!" In response to it I took refuge in one of the best hotels (so purported) until the sun, in its bright rays, should again start the world off right.

A splendid church for those days with a seating capacity for 175, and a school the like of which only few places in Oklahoma excelled, accommodating an hundred pupils. During the Christmas services of 1906 it was revealed that the capacity of the church would not accommodate the members of the congregation. The school attendance was also increasing and anticipating a further increase it would be impossible to accommodate them in the building.

The original church seated up to 350 after the 1907 expansion.

An addition to the church was therefore undertaken and on Jan. 30, 1907, the first load of material was brought on the grounds. On Feb, 9th the foundation was begun by Messsrs. Peter and J. Moran. As soon as this was completed the superstructure was begun.

The addition was a frame structure the same as the present church building and it more than doubled the capacity of the auditorium. Mr. H. Cupp had the supervision of the framework and he was assisted by many of the parishioners in the erection. By Maunday Thursday it was so far completed that it was pressed into service, and on Easter Sunday its capacity was tested.

While building the same, a parishioner said: "What is the use adding to this building? It will never be full anyhow. It is a waste of money and effort." He was told that it was hoped that his statement would prove wrong.

The stained glass windows which had been ordered for the addition encountered a wreck in transit and hence did never arrive but the order for same was duplicated at once, but made them so late that the church dedication date was at hand and the windows were not. Nevertheless the church was rededicated, because the addition was more than the original building, on the 17th day of April, 1907. The Rt. Rev. Theophile Meerschaert, D. D. dedicated it assisted by the clergy.

Immediately after the dedication solemn high mass was celebrated by Rev. Williard Woogden, O.S.B.of Perry, Okla., assisted by Father Dannis as Deacon and Father John Van den Hende as sub-deacon and Father Glynn as master of ceremonies. The Rt. Rev. Bishop preached the sermon on the "Church, the House of God."

The addition made the church cruciform and more than doubled the capacity.

The additional pews were manufactured by the Tulsa Planing Mill and harmonized with the pews therein. All were delighted to help the project with contributions and work. The sanctuary was beautified by a new altar at the cost of $600, which was the gift of the pastor. This completed the first step in the line of improvements.

On June 2nd of this year another class, after a thorough course of instruction, was admitted to First Holy Communion.

After due consideration since the 24th of May the second improvement was begun on the 3rd of June, when the first material for the foundation for the addition to the rectory was brought on the grounds.

On June 24, 1907 the foundation was completed and at the same time ground was broken for an extensive addition to the school building. Besides the other two additions, this meant an expenditure of more than $10,000.00.

The addition to the rectory came to a completion in September, at which time also the school should have been completed, but it had yet only reached the second story.

When school term opened in September not any of it could yet be utilized. In October we began to use the same partly but it was not completed until January, 1908. It was dedicated on the 31st of May, 1908.

This completed the three necessary improvements and it was hoped that it would serve us for a long time.

It gave the church and school ample capacity for the time being and externally they presented a much changed aspect.

When the church and school as to the exterior were completed and a well and a cistern had been completed to supply water, the interior furnishings had to be given further attention.

Two side altars were needed in the church to conform to the main altar. One of these was donated by the Altar Society and the other by Mr. John F. Black. The Altar Society also furnished the statue of the Blessed Virgin and the statue of St. Joseph was donated by Mr. and Mrs. Thomas Page.

A pulpit also was added which was donated by the Mr. E. J. Slater. The completion of the sanctuary furnishings was the sanctuary lamp donated by Mr. and Mrs. G. Forgue.

Two rooms in the rectory were furnished by Mr. P. Coyne. The altars and the pulpit were placed in the church in the Spring of 1908, in the latter part of April and the fore part of May.

All these improvements amounted to a very considerable sum, and created quite a debt; and the number of parishioners, was comparatively small. However, all were willing to do their respective share for they were beginning to realize the necessity of them and appreciate the expediency of the progress.

Accordingly, by Dec. 31, 1910, the entire indebtedness had been wiped out and additionally also Mother Catherine Drexel, who, as above stated, had advanced her money for the building of the school with the condition that it was to be returned when the school ceased to be an Indian school, had been settled with in full. This was due to the willingness and the generosity to promote the good work.

On May 31, 1908, the Rt. Rev. Bishop had again scheduled the Holy Family parish of Tulsa in his confirmation tour.

At this time the parish was increasing by leaps and bounds. By that time the oil industry had attracted the attention not only of those from other oil producing states, but quite from all states.

The church had not only been beautiful on the interior but unlike so many of the smaller churches, it had from the beginning artistic stained glass windows. In the original church the names of the donors as carried in the windows were: Rt. Rev. Theophile Meerschaert, Bishop; Rev. Charles Van Hulse; Family Appleby; Family Boyd; Collins, A. H.; Coyne, P. E.; Family Hoots; Family McLaughlin; Family Friend; Family Ririe. To these were added in the addition windows carrying the names of donors: John Constantine; Dr. C. A. Marshall; Agnes Hoots; Alfred Hoots.

On account of the influx of people an assistant was given me in the Rev. Father J. F. Davlin who arrived on the 25th of September, 1908. He was to attend to the various missions attached to this place. This condition was, however, of short duration, for the reason that there was a vacancy at Hartshorne and so the Rt. Rev. Bishop made him pastor there leaving here on the 19th of October, 1908. Rev. McManus succeeded him here, who arrived on the 26th of October this same year. He, too, became barely acquainted with the work of the missions when the Rt. Rev. Bishop was again compelled to appoint him pastor at Duncan, and at the same time appointing Rev. Joseph Van Eyck as the assistant here. This took place on February 5th, 1909. He remained in Tulsa until August 27th, when he was officially appointed pastor of Sacred Heart Church at Sapulpa, and was at the same time to attend to the missions which he was wont to attend to while here.

This left the Holy Family Parish only to my care until October 23rd, 1911, when Rev. John Van Gastel was appointed assistant. This was necessitated for the reason that the church could no longer accommodate the parishioners at two masses on Sunday and thus three were necessary.

With this arranged, some of the former missions were again attended to from Tulsa, which constituted part of the work of the assistant.

Parishioners brought their own shovels and carts to excavate the basement.

The year 1912 must stand out as one of note for the Holy Family Parish. In January, on the 29th, the Rt. Rev. again visited the parish and confirmed another class. A confirmation class is quite a barometer for the size of the parish and the membership of this class will show that the parish had increased remarkably.

1912 was not however prominent by reason of this only but also because after long delay during the whole of 1911, during which year a considerable part of the new church site was acquired, the work on the new church was begun.

The old church and school had been again outgrown by the parish and the old site had been hemmed in with surroundings not really compatible with the church and services and thus it became rather imperative to choose another site.

This necessitated very much additional expense but looking to the future, it seemed the only plausible thing to do.

The present site was selected and the greater part of it purchased at that time. It was in this year, upon approval of the plans by the Rt. Rev.

Bishop, that ground was broken on the octave of the feast of the Ascension of our Lord, it being the Feast of the Blessed Virgin Mary Help of Christians, May 23rd, 1912.

With no money on hand and with more than $30,000.00 debts because of the purchase of the lots, the undertaking appeared to be beyond accomplishment. Yet by the end of 1912 the foundation walls were rising above the ground, with the day in sight in the near future when the cornerstone should be blessed and laid.

Prior to this time the plans and specifications for the church had been approved by the Rt. Rev. Theophile Meerschaert, D. D. The evolution of this plan and style of church was rather novel. Father Heiring had drawn a rough pencil sketch presenting in outline the edifice which he considered befitting the Holy Family parish. This sketch with explanation he proposed to J. P. Curtin, an architect, associated with Winkler and MacDonald, who developed it into the plan of the present church. Mr. A. F. Wasielewski who specialized in church building, was given the work of executing the plan.

On the 28th day of September the concrete mixer was set in motion and the footings were poured as quickly as material could be handled. This was followed by the foundation walls and the other work without any cessation at any time until the completion of the building.

Rapid progress was made, and so, though the building was 200 feet long with 74 feet in nave and 94 in the transept, that by the first of February, 1913, the main floor was in and all was readiness for the laying of the cornerstone.

Amidst falling and drifting snow on the second of February, the feast of the Purification of the Blessed Virgin, 1913, the Stone was blessed and laid at 3 p. m. , by the Rt. Rev. Theophile Meerschaert, D. D., assisted by Rev. F. Van Mens, Rev. Edward Van Waesberge, Rev. Hubert Van Rechem, Rev. John Van Gastel, asst., and Rev. John G. Heiring, pastor.

Day by day the walls were growing and day by day the drain on the treasury became greater, however the progress of the work stimulated the interest in the work of the erection and the completion of the edifice, and as the interest grew so also the donations were increased. Yet so great was the strain that many a payday the builder, Mr. A. F. Wasielewski, personally carried over a considerable amount of the payroll.

Many a day were we perplexed to know whether we should be able to go on with the work, or should be compelled financially, to halt. Determination was accentuated by opposition at times as also by the hardship a halting would have imposed upon us.

The steel superstructure is enclosed in stone and brick.

By the 15th of August, 1913, the steelwork was completed and the work keeping pace with it. Having strained every effort and quite drained the avenues of finances by December 6th, 1913, we had so far succeeded that the cramped condition of our old quarters could be relieved. The building was now roofed and the basement in readiness for to hold services therein.

On the 5th and 6th of December all the furnishings were brought to the basement and on the 11th of December, being the Vigil of the Feast of the Immaculate Conception of the Blessed Virgin Mary and Sunday the first services were held there and the following day, the great feast of the Immaculate Mother of God was observed, the first feast in the church. Thenceforth the old church was used for school purposes, thus ample room being provided for the children.

This did not halt the work, but was prosecuted with vigor. The building exteriorly was not quite completed and the completion of the interior remained. Nevertheless, though in the winter months, the work could go on, unabated, and it did.

This rendered it possible to complete the church and have it in readiness for dedication by April 1, 1914.

The Dedication of Holy Family Church commenced after a parade from the old church to the new one. The parade included conventional and horseless carriages.

April 1, 1914, dawned in all the brightness and sweetness of Spring. On this day the old church on 3rd Street and Frankfort Ave., was closed and the new edifice opened by the solemn dedication of the same. The procession started at 9 A. M. and wended its way down Frankfort Avenue to Second Street, on Second to Main and South on Main Street to Eighth, and thence on Eighth to Boulder. The Stars and Stripes, with Tulsa Brass Band leading the way, followed by the Vested Servers Society, the Holy Childhood Association in white, and the girls of the school, the young ladies in autos, the Knights of Columbus, the Clergy and the Rt. Rev. Bishop in autos, followed by the city officials, Mayor and Commissioners, and other members of the congregation and citizens.

At ten o'clock the dedication took place. The Rt. Rev. Theophile Meerschaert dedicated the church assisted by the Rt. Rev. G. Depreitere, Rev. Hubert Van Rechem, Rt. Rev. John Metter, Rev. Urban de Hasque, Rev. F.

X. Van Mens, Rev. Fr. Casey, Rev. Fr. Tierney, Rev. John Van der Hende, Rev. J. F. McGuire, Rev. T. Coudron, Rev. Paul O.S.B., Rev. J. Davlin, Rev. Fr. Lamb, Rev. Jac. Van Gastel, Rev. Jos. Van Gastel, Rev. A. Suwalski, Rev. G. Geerer, O.S.B., Rev. A. Pierrets, Rev. John Van Gastel, Rev. J. Eloi, O.S.B., Rev. John G. Heiring.

Thus was completed the Tri-Spired Gem—the Holy Family Church of Tulsa, THE CITY'S PRIDE, THE CATHOLICS' BOON, THE HOUSE OF GOD AND OF BLESSINGS TO ALL.

The Holy Family Church was thus quite completely furnished in the interior and was also complete as to the exterior save for the time piece extending its hand to the four cardinal points to announce to the surroundings and vicinity the hours of both day and night.

The school, the great nursery of the Catholic church, next needed attention. After having transferred from the old location on Third Street, classes had been conducted quite successfully in what now is the Holy Family Parish Hall, St. Vincent de Paul Hall and other apartments, in the basement of the church.

However, it became very essential that a proper school building be erected so as to take care of the ever increasing number of pupils. Much relief was afforded both in the church and the school facilities in the year 1917, when, upon requests made to the Rt. Rev. Bishop, his Lordship in June of the same year officially made the division of the parish, by which all the territory lying east of the Midland Valley Railroad was to constitute a new parish.

Nothwithstanding this, a school was a necessity. Plans were therefore considered and perfected and in July, 1919, the excavation for the school building was begun. Simultaneously a new rectory was planned to supplant the old frame structure which was not adequate to house the priests. The excavations having been completed, the erection of these buildings was prosecuted with all possible energy. A. F. Wasielewski, who had erected the church, was also engaged to erect these. By the 13th of December the Rectory was so far completed as to permit the use of part of the same, necessitated by the fact that a severe cold wave freezing all the water pipes in the old house on temporary stilts rendered living in the same quite impossible.

May 30th, 1920, marked the formal opening of the rectory and the dedication of the Holy Family School. The intervening lot on the east side of the block having been purchased in February, 1920, the parish now owned the whole block minus the lot on the southeast corner.

This leaves the parish quite well equipped with up to date church, school and rectory.

The church extends its assistance not only to the living but also to the dead. This principally to the immortal souls by its prayers and especially the holy sacrifice of the mass by way of suffrage, but she is not unmindful of the body which has been inhabited by that soul and has been the temple of the Holy Ghost.

For this reason, the church places the bodies in blessed or consecrated graves, where they may rest until the angels trumpet shall summon them to judgment.

So in the Holy Family parish it was not sufficient to care for the living, but the dead had also to be cared for and as a consequence a fitting resting place was needed.

Up to 1910, circumstances so necessitating, interments were made in the city cemetery. In the spring of 1910 a 10-acre tract was acquired by the Holy Family parish, a little more than a mile beyond the city limits. This spot was prepared for burying ground as much as the limited means permitted. The difficulty of keeping it and improving the same was very much added to by the fact that the remains of many at that time were shipped to the former home of those who had located, at first thought, temporarily. As time went on, this practice was more and more abandoned, and, let it be said, to the advantage of all.

When, in the year 1917, the division of the parish took place, the east half of the cemetery was given to the new parish so as not to necessitate the purchase of another burying ground. Another site has been purchased for the reason that this plot is found too small, and is also being hemmed in too much with residences because of the growth and expansion of the city.

Also for the reason that the cemeteries may not be numerically increased as the city grows and the parishes become more numerous. The site now procured will serve the growing Catholic community for long years even though the population increase and the parishes be multiplied. It comprises 160 acres. The new location is eight miles further down the paved road and with the natural advantages there will make it, with proper care, a most beautiful city of the dead.

In the Spring and Summer of 1924 part of the 160 acres was platted and placed in readiness for interments. All remains were removed from the former cemetery as also the monuments, at the expense of the Catholic Cemetery Association (incorporated).

The Right Reverend Bishop has again seen it advantageous to divide the Holy Family Parish. That section of the city lying north of the Frisco Railroad and First Street running west from the intersection of it by the Frisco Railroad, and west of the Midland Valley Railroad constitutes the new parish under the title of "The Immaculate Conception Parish." Thus the Holy Family has been reduced very considerably in size and in the number of souls.

By the first of April, 1924, just ten years after the dedication of the church, the pastor hopes to see the parish financially unencumbered. He has, by reason of the material interests, not been able to give the intensity of his attention and interest to the spiritual welfare of the flock and of his own self as was his desire and might otherwise have been done. With these cares now considerably diminished, he hopes to intensify his efforts along spiritual lines, and he prays for intensified endeavors, along these lines on the part of the parishioners.

By one day's anticipation, the members of the Holy Family Parish, assembled in the Holy Family Parish Hall, changed into a banquet hall for the present, to commemorate the event of breaking of the ground for the Holy Family Church, which had taken place just, to the date, twelve years prior. It was on the Feast of our Lady Help of Christians. It was also commemorative of another event, which to the date, agreed with this former one, was the culmination of a campaign in which more than $100,000.00 were raised in six days for the payment of the indebtedness on the building.

This banquet was in itself an event, not commemorative, but celebrating the liquidation of all indebtedness of the parish, so that free from encumbrance it was in line to be consecrated. There was real cause for celebration and all who were present enjoyed the occasion. With well nigh one half million invested in church, school and rectory, and in its entirety paid for, was no little reason for joy and jubilation.

The Holy Family has also secured lots in West Tulsa, where, it is hoped, ere long a church as Mexican Mission will be erected. In concluding, let us pray that the history of the Holy Family parish may ever be bright and successful for the advancement of souls in the spiritual life and all for the greater honor and glory of God.

During this constructive period of the Holy Family Parish, Rev. J. Heiring, as pastor, was ably assisted by the Rev. J. F. Davlin from September 25, 1908 to October 19, 1908. By his promotion at such an early date to the pastorate of Hartshorne, Okla. his stay was short and he was replaced by the Rev. M. McManus on October 26, 1908. When he was promoted to the pastorate of Duncan, Okla. on February 9, 1909. Rev. Joseph Van Eyck took up the work on February 10, 1909 and continued so until August 29, 1909 when he was appointed pastor of Sacred Heart Parish of Sapulpa.

These Rev. Fathers were attending to the missions which were at that time connected with the Holy Family Parish and thus Holy Family Parish was left in charge of the pastor only.

This condition perdured until the parish membership had so increased that the space of the church would not accommodate them at two services on Sunday and a third mass became imperative.

To this end Rev. John Van Gastel was appointed assistant, who arrived on October 23, 1911. He spent part of his time and efforts in the parish and the other part of the time labored in the missions which were then again attached to the Holy Family Parish. At his appointment as pastor of St. Mary's Church of Guthrie, Okla., he was succeeded by Rev. D. C. Fletcher on July 1, 1917.

In December of 1919 Rev. D. C. Fletcher was appointed as pastor of Union City, Okla. This left the Holy Family Parish without a permanent assistant for the period intervening until the appointment of Rev. E. Depreitere February 4, 1920. During this time the Carmelite Fathers of Oklahoma City and Rev. E. Fontaine temporarily assisted.

During the absence of Rev. E. Depreitere for a visit to his home, Rev. H. Kickx and Rev. A. Hermann assisted on Sundays. He returned in October, 1920. In November 1922 he was appointed pastor of Bristow, Okla. and Rev. John J. Walde succeeded him in the Holy Family Parish. November 21, 1922. In August 1923 he was transferred to St. Joseph's Cathedral at Oklahoma City as assistant.

After that the Holy Family Parish was again without a permanent assistant until the appointment of Rev. Albert Achtergael on July 12, 1924.

Tulsa's Holy Family Church during the 1921 Tulsa Race Riot

by James O. Goodwin, Publisher,
Oklahoma Eagle; Lawyer; and
Parishioner, Holy Family Cathedral

This year marks the one hundredth anniversary of construction of Tulsa's Roman Catholic Holy Family Cathedral. The cathedral, parish school, and parishioners have lived through the joys and sorrows of Tulsa's everyday life, but they have also witnessed the dramas of the city's history. Among those dramas was the Tulsa Race Riot in 1921 -- a drama in which the church and its parishioners not only witnessed its horrors but acted with courage and compassion in ways that should inspire hope and pride for all Tulsans.

The facts of the riot and the explosive atmosphere of Tulsa's race relations in the 1920s bear remembering. When rumors spread through the city that a teenage white girl operating the elevator in the Drexel office building downtown had been assaulted by a black teenage boy (Dick Rowland), rioting by Tulsa's white population broke out and began a sixteen-hour reign of terror. The rioters invaded the black Greenwood area in Tulsa north – at that time the wealthiest black community in America -- and began their program of stealing, destroying, and killing – murdering men, women, and children. When the rioters had finished, almost 10,000 of the area's 11,000 residents were homeless. Two days later, knights of the Ku Klux Klan met on a hillside to celebrate the carnage by burning a large cross, a kind of trademark of the Klan. The Klan in those years rented space in Beno Hall, a hall that could seat 3500 people comfortably, located on Main Street just north of downtown. Beno Hall's name was said to be an acronym for "Be No Nigger, Be No Jew, Be No Catholic, and Be No Immigrant", and it was located on land owned by Tulsa founder, Democratic Party national committeeman, and Klan member Wyatt Tate Brady.

According to Tim Madigan's book The Burning, as the riot began, Holy Family Catholic School was having its graduation exercises at the convention hall (now known as the Brady Theater). In attendance were a thousand relatives and friends of Holy Family students, and on stage was seven-year-old Ruth Zigler Avery, who wore her new white dress. She was lined up across the stage with the other kids – arranged youngest to oldest. She had just finished speaking her single line from "The Nicest Dolly in all of the Town," when suddenly onto the stage came Father John Heiring, Holy Family's pastor. "I'm sorry," he said, "but everyone must take his children and return home immediately. A vicious race riot has erupted. Your lives are in great danger. When I am through with this announcement, please go straight home. Keep hold of your children's hands at all times. Do not drive with your lights on. When at home, pull down all of your window shades to keep anyone from seeing you. Use only candlelight. Do not leave your homes until advised by the newspapers that it is safe." With his right hand, Father Heiring made the sign of the cross: "May God bless you and keep you safe. In the name of the Father, the Son, and the Holy Ghost. Amen and goodbye."

Fleeing the hall, Ruth, her younger brother, and her aunt rushed to a trolley car stopped nearby. They immediately crouched down on the trolley's dirty floor, cutting their hands on glass there. (The trolley's car windows had already been shot out.) As the trolley took them towards their home, they remained on the floor in silence. Once arriving at eighth and Main Streets, they ran to their home a block away, got inside the house safely, pulled the curtains, and lit a small candle.

Ruth got into bed that night with her new white dress still on and lay in bed listening to the sounds of gunfire outside. Early the next morning, she heard an unusual sound -- trucks passing by the house. Peering carefully out the window, she saw two flatbed cattle trucks inching along. Dead bodies had been arranged, evidently in a hurry, on the flatbeds and on each other. She recalled afterwards seeing a woman's leg hanging from one of the flatbeds, and she said she wondered if it would topple onto the ground. And she saw the face on the body of a young boy – his eyes fixed open and his mouth gaping. She knew from talking before the riots with her Uncle Ross and Aunt Jesse that the Klan hated black people, and she naturally figured the Klan had killed the woman, the little boy, and the other black people stacked on the flatbed. She also said afterwards she could see that the dead boy on the flatbed was about her age, and she wondered if she might someday herself be put in a pile of bodies.

Not every white person in Tulsa participated in the riot, of course. But many of those who did not participate remained safely and silently in their homes. Only two white churches downtown opened their doors to shelter black refugees fleeing Greenwood: the Catholic Holy Family was one, the First Presbyterian was the other. According to an article published by the Tulsa Tribune on June 6, 1921, the Cathedral's nuns, its ladies of the St. Vincent de Paul Society, and its Knights of Columbus Council provided food, clothing, and shelter to four hundred black victims of the riot. Twenty-five babies were bathed and given clean clothes. Then on Wednesday following the riot, 250 meals were served to victims at the Cathedral. On Thursday, 150 meals were served. And on Friday, 75 meals were served. The Cathedral's ladies of the St. Vincent de Paul Society pledged as well to assist in the permanent relief and reconstruction of Tulsa north.

Mary Parish, who chronicled in a book the events of the riot, told about Mrs. George W. Hunt, a cosmetologist from Tulsa north, who credited her many white friends from the Holy Family for protecting her during the riot. Others were given refuge there and slept in the church basement. Among them were Wilhelmina Guess, her sister Bernice, her mother Minnie Mae, and her father the renowned attorney H.A. Guess, who valiantly helped to keep a lynch mob away from the teenage boy accused of assaulting the elevator operator. The nuns fed and clothed the Guesses, who in days following the riot had been interned along with hundreds of others in McNulty Park.

Aiding black victims of the riot was not free of risk for the Church and its parishioners in the 1920's. The message sought to be conveyed by rioters was that Tulsa's white society had no room for the black man, and the rioters' attitudes towards Catholics were little better. But the courage displayed by the people of Holy Family was a reply to the rioters' message. The Cathedral's people were saying that all men and women are children of God, entitled to receive the protection and help that all God's children deserve.

Tulsa and the Saint:
Katharine Drexel Slept Here

by Dr. Cherie Hughes

Tulsa has two distinctions few other U.S. cities can claim: A saint slept here, and she gave money to build what became Tulsa's Holy Family Cathedral School and Saint Monica's parish school. Her life's story not only provides an example of Christian faith in action, but has become part of the city's history and patrimony.

Katharine Drexel was born in 1859 into one of America's richest banking families. She and her two sisters grew up in privilege and luxury; they became debutantes, were educated at home by tutors, and were well traveled. But she also grew up in a household that took its religion seriously. The Drexel's Philadelphia home had an "oratory" – a room dedicated to morning and evening prayers --, and their summer country house had a chapel where a priest could celebrate Catholic mass. Her mother opened the back door of their home twice a week to meet with the poor who came to ask for clothing, food, coal for fuel, medicine, shoes, and occasionally a burial fee. Mrs. Drexel called her personal charity "Dorcus", after the woman in Acts of the Apostles who sewed clothes for poor widows, and the three Drexel girls helped in their mother's Dorcus work by keeping a diary of what was given and to whom. The petitioners coming to the Drexels' back door grew so large in numbers the family had to hire a policeman for crowd control. Charity was something the future saint learned at her mother's knee. And charity was not just giving out necessities and money; as young teenagers, Katharine and her sisters taught Sunday School at the all-Black St. Peter Claver parish in Philadelphia.

The plight of the country's Native Americans came to her attention early through a family friend who later served as her spiritual advisor, Fr. James O'Connor, who became Bishop of Nebraska Territory and then the Diocese of Omaha. In the 1880s, the Drexel sisters toured Indian missions of the Sioux, Arapahoe, Crow, and Shoshone tribes in Bishop O'Connor's diocese. Struck by the great need she saw, Katharine Drexel gave money to the Indian missions in annual amounts starting at $500 but within five years was over $80,000. By 1890, she had funded missions and schools stretching from Seattle in the Pacific Northwest to Mexico and including schools for Oklahoma's Cherokee, Creek, Comanche, and Osage.

As a young girl, Katharine had dreamed of living her life as a cloistered, contemplative nun. But with her wealth, social standing, and beauty, eligible young men often were her suitors. It was a life she enjoyed -- but not the life she wanted. Instead, during a private audience with Pope Leo XIII, when she asked the Holy Father to send priests for Bishop O'Connor's Indian missions, the pope responded by asking her to become a missionary herself. She had wanted to serve destitute Native Americans, but she had not seen herself as missionary!

And she faced this dilemma: If she became a nun, the superiors of her order would have rights to control her money, and if she married, her husband would have rights to control her money. It took her six years to convince her skeptical friend Bishop O'Connor of the seriousness of her calling, but once convinced he urged her to found her own missionary order. She spent twenty months in a Pittsburgh convent of the Sisters of Mercy learning about the nun's life. And in 1891, she became the first sister in her own new order and its first superior. To the traditional vows of poverty, chastity, and obedience, she added a fourth, which she described in the language of the day, to be "a mother and servant to the Indians and Colored People."

Most of her new order's earliest missions were intended for Native Americans, because she feared that their small numbers would cause them to be overwhelmed by concerns for the larger numbers of Blacks in need. But even within her order, things changed, and its Black missions eventually outnumbered missions for Native Americans. The Sisters of the Blessed Sacrament for Indians and Colored People built more than twenty-two Black schools in south Louisiana alone, including Xavier University – the only university in the U.S. that is both historically Black and Catholic.

In addition to Blessed Sacrament missions and schools, Katharine Drexel continued to contribute money to other Indian and Black schools served by religious orders not her own. Accordingly, Oklahoma's bishop Theophile Meerschaert convinced her to build a school in Tulsa. Until the old Holy Family Church opened its doors in 1899, the town's Catholics had met in private homes for mass. At the same time as a modest wooden church was being built at what is now Third and Elgin in Tulsa, Drexel monies ($1,500) were used to build what was then called St. Theresa's Institute for Indian Girls adjacent to the new church.   By year's end, St. Theresa's had eighty students, only twenty were Holy Family parishioners. When the school eventually became the parish school and ceased being for Indian girls exclusively, the name changed to Holy Family School and the Drexel funds were repaid. (Katharine Drexel had insisted that her money was only to benefit those of her specific apostolate – support for Blacks and Indians – and that if a facility should change its mission the money had to be repaid for use elsewhere.) Eventually, Drexel funds helped to build every Catholic Indian and Black school in Oklahoma.

Her apostolate to be mother and servant to Indians and Blacks made her many friends, but also some enemies.   When her order was getting ready to move into its permanent motherhouse in Pennsylvania, the Ku Klux Klan there welcomed it by burning a cross on convent grounds and promising to blow the place up.   And Klan members in Beaufort, Texas, tarred and feathered the father of one of her students, threatening to burn down the school. The sisters prayed for protection, and a small tornado soon destroyed completely the Beaufort Klan meeting house.   To some, the tornado was a fortuitous coincidence, but others saw it as divine intervention.   And when the Klan supported Tulsa's 1921 race riot, Katharine Drexel responded by building a school for Tulsa's new Black parish of St. Monica's.

For her genuine affection and care for Indians and Blacks and for her virtues of generosity and piety, the Catholic Church declared her a saint on October 1, 2000. She is the only canonized saint to have visited Tulsa, which she did regularly on trips to inspect the missions and schools she had built.   When in town, she stayed with sisters who taught at what is now called Holy Family Cathedral School, on the top floor of the school's present building at eighth and Boulder.   The Holy Family Cathedral should have a plaque that says "Katharine Drexel slept here" – or, better, "Saint Katharine Drexel slept here."

Holy Family School
by Mrs. Kay Keith

Mother Katharine Drexel

In the mid 1890's, Catholics in Tulsa petitioned **Most Reverend Theophile Meerschaert**, Bishop of Indian Territory, to create a school for their small town. He sought the aid of **Mother Katharine Drexel,** the famous millionaire nun. She donated $1,500 toward the construction of the first Catholic school in Tulsa, provided it was called St. Therese's Institute and focused on educating Native American girls. The bishop agreed.

Tulsa's First Catholic School

Bishop Meerschaert purchased land at Third and Elgin and began building a small church and school. The first Mass was said at Holy Family Church on Sunday, September 10, 1899. Because construction of the school was behind schedule, classes were held inside the church beginning on Monday September 11, 1899. There were 80 students at that time.

When the parish repaid Mother Drexel in 1902, they were then free to choose the new name of Holy Family School. By 1910, fueled by the growth of the oil industry, the Tulsa population had grown to 18,000. The parish outgrew its facilities and, led by their pastor, Reverend John G. Heiring, they began planning for a new church and school at Eighth Street and Boulder, located on the outskirts of Tulsa. The new school was dedicated in 1920 and from that time until 1960 the school was teeming with several hundred students.

Tough Times

In 1960, the new diocesan high school Bishop Kelley was opened, necessitating the closing of both Holy Family and Marquette High Schools. With the closing of the high school and the movement of parishioners to the suburbs, enrollment at Holy Family dwindled and the decline continued for many years. There was talk of closing the school because the parish could not sustain it. At this time, Holy Family became a diocesan school.

The Rebirth of the School

Then in 1996, **Bishop Edward J. Slattery** invested over $1,600,000 to bring the building into good repair. The school was soon returned to the parish, under the leadership of **Monsignor Gregory A. Gier,** Rector of the Cathedral. A new era began. In the intervening years, the school has experienced a renaissance. The school now serves students from a diverse cultural base that are excelling academically and are learning and living their faith.

This bit of history illustrates Holy Family Cathedral and its school's unique connection to both the city of Tulsa and the Catholic community. For over a century, thousands of young people have been prepared spiritually and academically to become life-long participants in the life of the church and the civic community. Its importance to the City of Tulsa is beyond measure. All Catholics of this diocese can take pride in Holy Family Cathedral and Holy Family Cathedral School.

Catholics Serving in the Military during Wartime

an interview with Reverend Colonel Jerry Mattox, USAF
and CDR Mark Nelson, USN, Retired

by Michael A. Malcom

"Is it a mortal sin to kill somebody during a war?" asked a thoughtful high school student in my Confirmation class. We had been discussing the importance of going to Confession. Everyone in the class agreed that while maintaining a state of grace is essential, our fallen human nature leads us to sin - sometimes breaking one of the Ten Commandments.

I replied to the student, "We have a deacon in the parish who was a fighter pilot in the Vietnam war. Why don't you ask him after class?"

Reverend Colonel Jerry Mattox, USAF, better know to us as Deacon Jerry, is a retired Air Force pilot and engineer. His education in Theology plus his experience as a military man makes him a good resource for tough questions.

I interviewed Deacon Jerry and CDR Mark Nelson, USN, Retired, to get their thoughts on being Catholic and serving in the military during wartime.

When did you serve? Where?

Mark Nelson: I served in the Pacific Theater starting in 1952. My main job - as an enlisted man - was an engineer working on boilers on a tanker. I was part of the crew that loaded and offloaded the tanker. We took oil to Japan, Alaska, and didn't bring much back with us. We picked up most of our oil on Long Beach and Aruba and took it to American bases to resupply their fuel oil for Navy ships, and aviation fuel. We also replenished ships at sea.

Deacon Jerry Mattox: I joined the Air Force in 1963, got a commission immediately and went through pilot training. I flew various fighters for the next twenty-five years. I flew the F-100 in Vietnam, the F-104 in Florida, and the F-4E in Germany. I managed to get promoted along the way and retired as a Colonel.

How was your military experience of Catholicism different from parish life?

Deacon Jerry Mattox: The big difference that I see is that in the military, if a senior officer tells you to do something, you do it. Here - even in the Church - it either doesn't happen at all or it doesn't happen to the same degree even if the priest or bishop has a different point of view.

Mark Nelson: My experience is the same. During my first job as the executive officer of a ship, we were assigned to do a certain task. I told the captain - diplomatically, of course - we really shouldn't be doing this. He said, "Here's a word of advice: you can get to the point where you want to make that statement and **should** make it. But when a senior officer says, 'Do it,' you do it."

How did your experience vary from country to country?

Deacon Jerry Mattox: The Catholic Church is everywhere that I have been. That's a great comfort to me, particularly having a priest nearby - even in a Quonget hut in Foo Kat. We had daily Mass. It was comforting to go to Mass before we went out into combat.

The universal Church is the universal Church. When I was in the military, everything was fully orthodox so there really wasn't much of a difference in the Church from country to country. American soldiers, for the most part, are not Catholic. We were definitely in the minority.

For some, life in the military includes certain activities that Catholics can't participate, for example, some of the drinking bouts and other activities. But it's not much different from our secular life today.

What interaction did you have with clergy?

Deacon Jerry Mattox: The Air Force, because we were in major bases, there was almost always easy access to a priest. I don't think it was that way for Mark.

Mark Nelson: No, it was the opposite! There was usually never a priest. But because I was Catholic, I always found a place to go to Mass whenever we pulled into port. When I served, Mass was in Latin. No matter where I was, Mass was the same everywhere. Even in Vietnam, our base was fairly large, but we often didn't see a priest.

One of the things that impressed me was that the Navy bosses tried to find a priest to come to the ship to say Mass for us, or they would make arrangements for us to go to Mass when we came to a port. I saw a lot of friends get "lost in the shuffle" because they didn't have regular contact with their clergy. Many of my Catholic friends maintained their faith because they just did it - they went to Mass even when it meant a sacrifice of not being able to go to shore - especially on weekends, on Sundays. I did what I could to invite the enlisted men's families to come on board to attend Mass.

Do you have a message for young Catholics considering military service?

Deacon Jerry Mattox: The military is a wonderful way of life for a single man. If you're married, it's very difficult to maintain a successful marriage because you're separated so much and so often. Marriages don't work well when you're separated, particularly if there are children. That needs to be uppermost in a young man's or young woman's mind.

The second point is that you are joining a family that takes care of it's own and does a pretty good job of it, but the mores are not Catholic. There is an attitude towards alcohol and sex and language that doesn't match well with the Catholic Faith. A young man should be aware of that and should know that he should not participate fully in that society.

Mark Nelson: The biggest problem with respect to marriage is that there is always a temptation to do whatever everybody else does when they go on shore leave. It's not easy to break away from your buddies and say, "I don't want to do that tonight. I'm not going to do that."

What was the most rewarding part of your service?

Mark Nelson: Working on an aircraft carrier! I maintained the first optical glide path system that helped planes land on the deck of the carrier. I was given a piece of equipment without an instruction book and no spare parts and was told, "Keep it running." I was able to do that.

The pilots were afraid that if the optical mirror somehow went awry, it would be a safety issue. I felt so sure that this system was working well, that I would be glad to ride in one of the first airplanes landing on the carrier. Before I installed the optical system, our carrier had four or five flight deck crashes. Afterwards, we didn't have any crashes. The Navy was pretty well pleased with it.

The company that built the system came aboard and asked us why our system was still working while other units on other carriers had stopped. The warrant officer pointed to me and said, "It's because of *this guy.*"

Another rewarding moment was while I was on the carrier. I was approached by a Marine Captain in charge of the Marine Guard. He thought that I had some real leadership capabilities because I started a Catholic Choir and helped the Protestants get their choir started. I put the two groups together and we learned a couple of patriotic songs that we'd sing on one of the elevators as we pulled into port. The Captain of the ship thought that was pretty good, so he sent me to Officer Candidate School. That's how I got my commission.

Deacon Jerry Mattox: I have an experience, rather than a single moment. It is the blending of the pilot's personality with the fighter aircraft. It doesn't happen immediately; it takes some time for it to happen, but it is one of the big attractions in flying single-seat airplanes. Every fighter pilot I know has experienced it or he doesn't continue to fly single-seat airplanes.

Restorations and Renovations

by Michael A. Malcom

The three best ways to get unsolicited advice is to purchase a house, to have a baby, and to renovate a church. Many of us are familiar with the first two; the latter is a rather uncommon experience.

Monsignor Gregory Gier arrived in 1997 as the new rector of Holy Family Cathedral. Before he finished his first year, he began exploring the idea of renovating the Cathedral. "Renovating" wasn't his word; he preferred "restoration."

Many churches in the late 1960s and early 1970s underwent renovations to conform to many of the liturgical changes following the Second Vatican Council. Often those renovations included removing various elements of the church. Dismayed parishioners recount leaving a familiar and comfortable church one Sunday only to return the next to a stark and cold "renovated" church.

Holy Family went through a renovation in the late 60s and early 70s. The sanctuary was expanded into the center of the cruciform at the price of eliminating the communion rail and pulpit that wrapped around one of the church's pillars.

The original pulpit and winding staircase wrapped around a pillar.

The wrap-around pulpit had been installed in the church a few years after its 1914 dedication. Some members of the building committee expressed their concern that speech intelligibility would suffer in a church with such high Gothic arches. They were right. On the other hand, choirs love to sing in Holy Family precisely because of that extraordinary reverberation.

The pulpit featured a sounding-board that helped to direct the sound of the homilist's voice to the people in the pews. While not perfect, parishioners were content with the clarity of the spoken word.

No one recorded why the pulpit was moved from its original pillar to the one on the right. That move, plus several decades of priests walking up and down the steps, aged the pulpit's *scagliola* compound (marble dust mixed with an adhesive) resulting in some cracks and structural weakening. The pulpit's removal was a sad occasion, but understandable.

While many churches removed theirs, Holy Family's three reredos altars remained in place. They had been purchased by the parish shortly after the church opened its doors. Still paying off the construction debt, the parish saved its money to purchase the central high altar in 1915 for $2,000 from the Deprato Company. Two years later, both side altars were purchased and installed at a cost of $800 each.

Over the two following decades, the church grew full of canvas paintings glued to the walls and colorful statues on pedestals. Cherubs painted on the ceiling flew from cloud to cloud. The vision of the church's builders had been realized.

The 1948 Renovation

By the mid-1940s, the bright pastel tones that had been so popular when Holy Family was built had fallen out of favor. Parishioners wished for greater visual interest. They would be happy to donate towards a newly designed interior.

Lighting technology had changed radically since the gas lights were hung in the church in the 1910s. New brassy chandeliers hung from the underside of each arch in the nave. Small lights illuminated the angels and saints in the high altar.

The once-beautiful wooden floor aged rapidly. While many of the choices made in 1948 had a goal of upgrading Holy Family's appearance, it was determined that the floor was not to receive so nice a treatment. It was replaced with faux-marble linoleum.

Holy Family's interior glows as new electric lights replace gas lamps.

The walls of the church were painted with a fresh base coat of paint and finished with an ornate set of stencils. The vaulted ceiling above the apse received a blue-green and gold vine pattern, one so well liked that it survived the next two renovations.

In the next couple of decades, air cooling technology advanced. Two sets of windows in the upper church were removed so that a new pair of air coolers could lower the temperature of Holy Family on hot summer days. The church's coal burning boiler was converted to run on natural gas.

The church began to experiment with electric sound systems. Nothing satisfactory was installed for decades.

The 1974 Renovation

In the parish's early history, Tulsa's tremendous growth was good for the parish. The church had been surrounded by houses. Neighborhood kids had walked to school every day. Families strolled around the church every evening.

By the 1960s, Tulsa had begun to grow beyond Holy Family. Developers bought entire blocks of houses to raze them and build up Tulsa's skyline with large office buildings. Retail stores and shopping centers in downtown closed and moved to the suburbs.

Holy Family High School and Christ the King's Marquette High School closed in 1960. The students at both schools transferred to the new Bishop Kelley High School.

Holy Family parish had been split many times to create Christ the King, Saint Monica, Saint Catherine, Saint Augustine, the Madalene, Saint Mary's and several other new parishes. Most Tulsans were moving further away from downtown and attended local parishes rather than driving downtown.

The 1960s were a grim time in Holy Family's history. The parish was fortunate to have had a number of dedicated pastors and parishioners.

Now half a century old, the church building was beginning to need repairs and maintenance to its interior and exterior. Without a large budget, the parish replaced crumbling mortar in the brickwork and stonework. The interior walls, cracked during the construction of nearby skyscrapers, were painted in simple, cheerful colors inspired by the stained glass windows.

The elevation of Holy Family to the status of *cathedral* in 1973, coupled with the expanded sanctuary following the Second Vatican Council, had a profound impact on the church's interior. The sanctuary was reconfigured with the bishop's chair in the apse. The Blessed Sacrament was reserved in the side altar of the Blessed Virgin. The new altar stood in the middle of the cruciform so that the entire presbyterate of the new diocese could concelebrate the Eucharist with their bishop.

New carpet quieted the sound of feet shuffling forward during Communion. Padded kneelers replaced wooden ones. Custom wooden doors provided quiet in the confessionals.

During this time, Holy Family Cathedral set itself apart from other Catholic parishes. Long lines in front of the confessionals had become normal. The church's soaring arches made it a popular church for weddings. Even though fewer Tulsa Catholics regularly attended Mass there, Holy Family was the place where memories were being made.

Men climb scaffolding to paint the trim around clerestory windows.

In the early 1990s, new white marble replaced carpet in the sanctuary. The Sacred Heart altar, consecrated by the cardinal archbishop of New York in 1925 and sitting in the sacristy for years, was refinished and moved into the church as the new main altar. Other marble pieces recovered from the Sacred Heart altar were assembled into a new ambo.

The Recent Renovation

The most recent renovation was conceived in a number of Parish Council meetings in the late 1990s. Monsignor Gier had at first the goal of replacing the Cathedral's aluminum roof, but like many building projects, that one goal became part of a long list of proposed improvements to the church.

Ninety years of Oklahoma thunderstorms and rains aged the roof, its decking, and major structural beams in the church. Much of the church's wiring was outdated and needed to be replaced. There had never been a handicapped accessible restroom on the pew level. After many failed experiments with a variety of products, the church needed a good sound system.

Reviewing the quickly growing list, Monsignor Gier prioritized the needs of the Cathedral. He made it clear that this was a *restoration* rather than a *renovation*. The goal was to use modern construction materials and technology to replace and, if possible, hide visible modern intrusions into our 1914 church. He asked if there is a way to remove the thirty-six loudspeakers in the church. He wondered if all fourteen rectangular air conditioning registers could be disguised.

2006

In 2006, the first act of the construction crew was to remove the basket of speakers, semi-affectionately known as the "coffee filter." A month after it was installed in the 1990s, the hope of getting it to work was abandoned, yet the basket remained.

At the Easter Vigil in 2006, after an unusually large number of people were baptized, received into the Catholic Faith, and confirmed, Monsignor Gier returned the Eucharist to the tabernacle in the center of the high altar in the apse. The bishop's *cathedra* was moved to a prominent place at the side of the apse. The sanctuary lamp was suspended from the vaulted ceiling above the apse.

The removal of the basket of speakers was the first act of the Restoration.

Parishioners were enthusiastic about the changes. This *restoration* was indeed a restoration.

The rotten end of a wooden beam needed immediate replacement.

Following these conspicuous changes, work moved into the church's attic. A series of beams mounted end to end supported the apex of the roof over the main aisle of the church. Water damage led to decay at one end of the beam causing it to fall six inches. Workers raised it back into place and secured it in a steel boot. They installed braces along the length of the beam, ensuing that none but the most violent of Oklahoma's storms will ever shake the beam again.

In the summer of 2006, a set of stairs leading from one of the front entrances to the choir loft was rerouted to make space for a large restroom suitable for use by persons in wheelchairs or to a parent with children.

Later that summer, the air conditioner registers were removed and filled in with drywall and plaster. New holes were made in the plaster walls. They were covered with large plaster disks, called roundels. The roundels served two purposes: they allowed cool air to flow into the Cathedral without looking as industrial as their preceding rectangular registers, and they mimicked the church's round canvas paintings that hung in 1914.

Perforated plaster roundels hid the rectangular air conditioning vents.

Specialists in fire prevention drilled holes in the vaulted ceiling and installed water pipes and sprinkler heads. This fire suppression system dramatically lowered the cost of insurance.

2007

In March, Father Matthew La Chance, associate pastor, former architect, and indispensable advisor to the rector, placed glass panels in the wooden interior doors leading into the church. At the same time carpet in the vestibules was removed, revealing a tile floor. Painters tested colors on the vestibule walls for later use in the church.

Work on the fire suppression system continued. Finished in October, it was one of the most advanced systems in Tulsa. While many systems are full of water at all times, the pipes at Holy Family sit empty. In the case of a fire, water pressure expels the air from the empty pipes, causing the sprinkler heads to extend down into the interior of the Cathedral and quickly extinguish any fire.

Glass inserts in the doors bring additional light into the entrances.

The interior of the central spire - itself ten stories tall - contains a large spiral staircase.

2008

The church's original red slate roof was replaced with aluminum in the late 1950s. Aluminum, the church was promised, was the best roofing material because it would *never* wear out. Holy Family parish felt quite secure it was using the best available materials.

We now know that aluminum is a terrible roofing material. While it is initially resistant to hail storms, the metal ages rapidly and loses its resilience. As soft drink cans on the side of the road become brittle, so do aluminum shingles.

In the late 1990s, the shingles had become so brittle that every thunderstorm blew at least a few shingles off the Cathedral's roof. A couple of especially powerful storms blew away sections of shingles exposing the decking.

The most alarming problem happened during windstorms. The wooden decking under the shingles had rotted. Nails and rivets that once held the wood tightly to the steel superstructure lost their grip. It was frightening to see more than one hundred square feet of decking and shingle lift slightly off the building's frame.

The parish had purchased extra shingles in 1958, but had run out of replacements by this time. A company in Canada agreed to manufacture new aluminum replacements, but when they were installed they were so shiny that Cathedral workers sprayed gray paint on them to dull them and match the rest of the roof.

The Cathedral's shiny aluminum roof began to dull in the 1980s and 1990s.

New copper graces the lower roof while bare decking on the spires awaits a roof.

In 2008, roofers stripped the aluminum shingles off the spires. They removed the plywood decking and rebuilt the spires with metal materials. Shiny new copper shingles were installed on the lower sections of roof and on the two smaller spires. Daily visible progress brought lots of attention from news outlets.

The Chapel of Peace was created in the 1970s as an alternative to using the church for daily Mass. By this time, very few families lived in downtown, but the number of Catholics working in downtown offices had grown considerably. They had attended Mass in the church and in a small building south of the School.

The Chapel is nearly gutted before it is rebuilt.

The Chapel was decorated in a minimalist, unassuming style. Chairs with armrests and kneelers in the back provided seating for about thirty. An altar, ambo, chair, and credence table sat upon a raised, carpeted platform.

After three decades, several chairs had broken and the rest had grown uncomfortable. The walls, carpet, and drop ceiling needed replacement. The decision was made to redecorate with modern materials in the style of a 1914 chapel. Wood flooring would grace the platform as tin ceiling tiles hung overhead. Energy efficient lighting replaced outdated incandescents.

The completed Chapel continues to serve Catholics who work in downtown Tulsa.

2009

When the small parish of Saint Henry in Plunketville, Oklahoma closed, the pews were donated to Holy Family with the intention of putting them in the Chapel. Not only were these pews a welcome donation, they represented a reunion of sorts. The priest who built Holy Family Cathedral took vacations in Plunketville. He founded Saint Henry Parish and stayed in a small cottage on the church grounds. The pews were the last addition to the updated Chapel.

No part of the restoration was as controversial as the colors of the paint on the interior of the church. Inspired by the brightest colors from the stained glass windows, the appearance of vivid hues was shocking at first - especially to parishioners who were familiar with only the 1974 placid color scheme. Long time parishioners commented that it reminded them of how the church looked during their childhood.

The apse of the Cathedral is filled with scaffolding.

While other churches closed during their renovations, Holy Family Cathedral was open every Sunday. Parishioners walked around a very large blue crane and lost sight of the high altar when it was obscured by a seventy foot tall scaffolding.

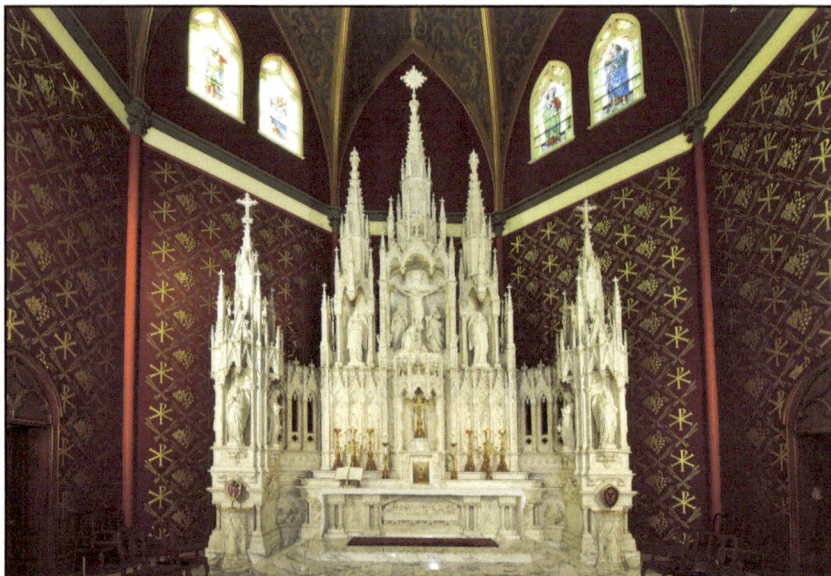

Chi-Rhos, Grapes, and Wheat stencils over a wine red base accentuate the high altar's centerpiece: Christ Crucified.

The Cathedral's columns were painted a vibrant orange-red to echo columns found in the bases of the church's stained glass windows. Yellows and greens replaced quiet pastels on the lower and upper walls.

While the scaffolding was in place in the apse, two painters retraced the beautiful vine pattern with blue-green and gold paint.

The walls behind the three reredos altars had previously been painted a light gray. The white altars seemed to disappear in front of the light wall behind it.

Consideration was given to using rich colors on those walls to increase the contrast between them and the altars. The high altar's centerpiece is Christ's Death on the Cross. The red paint was inspired by the robes Jesus wears in two stained glass windows: *The Wedding Feast at Cana* and *Jesus Giving the Keys to the Kingdom to Saint Peter*. The red paint is an especially close match to the water-turned-to-wine in the Cana window.

The left side altar is dedicated to the Blessed Virgin Mary. Inspired by one of seven windows of Saint Mary, the one high above that altar, the hues of Mary's robes influenced the Marian blue on the nearby walls.

The right side altar depicts Saint Joseph as the patron saint of a happy death. Saint Joseph, in a stained glass window above the marian altar, is robed in an African violet. The saturated purple tones in the painted walls were markedly different from the earlier soft yellows.

The lively red and blue and purple walls remained unadorned for about a year. A couple of families in the parish paid for a costly yet beautiful stenciling to go over the red apse wall. The church hired a well known and widely praised specialist from Kansas to apply the stencils. He used a thick gold paint to create the shapes of wheat and grapes, symbols of the Eucharist. He painted the Chi-Rho, the monogram of Christ in Greek.

With a few weeks, other parishioners donated the stenciling on the walls behind the two side altars. Roses and the initials for *Ave Maria* accompany the Altar of the Blessed Virgin. The fleur-de-lis, a stylized Easter Lily, the tools of a carpenter and a "J" for Joseph grace the walls near Saint Joseph's altar.

Artist Tim Linenberger stencils a frieze pattern under the clerestory.

Attention turned toward the walls of the transepts and nave. A criticism of the 1974-2006 palette of colors was that the eye was not drawn heavenward as the first two iterations of the interior did. An imbrication, a repeating series of shapes, was chosen to give height to the walls. The imbrication chosen was a series of rectangles with a small quarter-circle in the corner.

In late Summer, with the copper roof completed, men on cranes returned to Holy Family to paint the metal finials atop the battlements crowning the church's towers. They painted the clock faces and the louvers a brilliant white, similar to the original 1914 colors.

2010-2014

With the major work having been completed, smaller projects were given attention as money came available. While many parishioners had donated towards a major fund drive, others chose to donate to a monthly *Building the Future* collection. Monies from this fund paid for a final set of stencils in a frieze pattern that run around the perimeter of the upper church.

The priests' sacristy was painted. New lighting, refinished wood floors, rugs, and new cabinets give the room a brighter and cleaner appearance.

Conclusion

Holy Family Church has been host to thousands of Baptisms, Confirmations, Confessions, and Weddings. How many souls have attended Mass there in these one hundred years? How many newly ordained priests have turned to their bishops to offer a first blessing?

Each of those experiences involves a moment of grace from God. They often create an emotional connection that binds us to the place where the experience took place.

Holy Family Church is fortunate to have had a number of bishops and rectors who actively cared for the Christian Faithful and the church in which they pray. These shepherds have preserved the "Tri-Spired Gem" for our generation and for future ones.

The Church at Prayer

In order for the parishioners of the Cathedral to better understand the reasons why Bishop Slattery chose to begin celebrating the Novus Ordo Mass *ad orientem*, the following essay was published in the parish newsletter and bulletin in Advent of 2009:

One of the fundamental characteristics of Catholic worship is the understanding that the Mass is our offering of Christ's sacrifice to the Father. We do this in union with Christ and as members of his Body (through Baptism.) In offering this sacrifice, the priest stands 'in the person of Christ,' the historic head of his mystical Body.

From the most ancient times, the position of the celebrant and the congregation reflected the meaning of the prayers they offered, since the people prayed, standing or kneeling, in the place which visibly represented Our Lord's Body, while the priest at the altar stood in representation of Christ, the Head. Everyone - celebrant and congregation - stood in the same direction, offering to the Father the one and same Sacrifice which Christ offered upon the cross.

This single position is called *ad orientem* or 'towards the east' since in the ancient tradition of the Church, the priest and the people all prayed to the east, in the expectation that when Christ returns to us, He will return 'from the east.' At Mass, we stand - vigilant and waiting for that return - even as we offer to the Father the Sacrifice of Christ's life, death and resurrection.

For the past forty years, however, the priest and the people have been set to face in opposite directions. This practice was introduced after the Council, partly to help the people understand the liturgical action of the Mass and partly as an accommodation to the culture of our times in which people who exercise authority are expected to face directly the people whom they serve.

Unfortunately this change had a number of unforeseen and negative effects. First of all, it was a serious rupture with the venerable tradition of the Church. Secondly, it often gave the appearance that the priest and the people were engaged in a conversation *about* God, rather than the worship *of* God.

This in turn made it more difficult to understand the true nature of the Mass, that is, the sacrificial nature of the Mass. And finally, it placed too much importance on the personality of the priest by placing the celebrant on a kind of liturgical stage.

Our Holy Father, Pope Benedict XVI urges us to draw upon the ancient liturgical practice of the Church in order to foster a deeper and more authentic Catholic worship, and for that reason, Bishop Slattery began the practice of celebrating the 10:00 Mass *ad orientem*, that is, facing the same direction as the Faithful do at Mass.

Our late Holy Father, Pope John Paul II, worked tirelessly to call the world's attention to the Mystery of Christ present and manifest in his Body, the Church. Pope Benedict continues to teach that when we become members of Christ's Body through Baptism we receive a mission from Christ to transform our world in His image by our faith, hope and charity.

This transformation of our world and our culture to better reflect the image of Christ is what John Paul called 'the New Evangelization.' Central to this New Evangelization is the public, liturgical prayer of the Church, which is our worship of the Father through the Sacrifice of the Mass and the daily celebration of the Liturgy of the Hours.

Despite the great diversity of our prayers and devotions, the Catholic liturgy has always maintained a marvelous adherence to the Apostolic Tradition of the Church's life. Pope Benedict has made the recovery of this rich tradition a constant feature of his pontificate. One important part of the Church's ancient liturgical practice is the celebration of the Mass *ad orientem*, that is, with both the celebrant and the congregation facing in the same direction.

Why restore the practice? First of all because it better represents what the Mass is all about. It shows - quite visibly - that the people and the priest are united in a single action, offering one sacrifice, but offering it in their proper roles, the people joined to Christ as his Body and the priest configured to Christ as the Head of the Body.

Secondly, this ancient practice avoids the impression that the priest and the congregation are engaged in a conversation *about* God, rather than the worship *of* God.

Thirdly, the celebration of the Mass *ad orientem* reduces the temptation to regard the priest as a kind of actor playing a sacred role on a liturgical stage, by restoring in a clear fashion what his priestly role is: the one who stands in the person of Christ in the offering of Our Lord's Body and Blood to the Father.